BLUE JUNGLE

BLUE JUNGLE

Nadolyn H. Robinson

Copyright © 2022 by Nadolyn H. Robinson.

All rights reserved. No part of this book may be reproduced in any form or by any electronic or mechanical means, including information storage and retrieval systems, without permission in writing from the publisher, except by reviewers, who may quote brief passages in a review.

ISBN: 978-1-957054-21-6 (Paperback Edition)
ISBN: 978-1-957054-22-3 (Hardcover Edition)
ISBN: 978-1-957054-20-9 (E-book Edition)

Some characters and events in this book are fictitious. Any similarity to the real persons, living or dead, is coincidental and not intended by the author.

Book Ordering Information

Phone Number: 315 288-7939 ext. 1000 or 347-901-4920
Email: info@globalsummithouse.com
Global Summit House
www.globalsummithouse.com

Printed in the United States of America

Contents

Translucent 1

The Color Of Love 4

The Lazarus Effect 7

Leader Bandit 10

Heaven Is Real 11

Blue Jungle 13

Dulce 15

Judgement 17

Who's Fool/ You're Fool/ No Fool You're Game/ No Name /
    Period 19

It Is True 20

Fortitude 21

Someday 22

Waiting For The Season Yet To Come 23

Silence 25

Crucified 28

Space 29

Words Of Wisdom Extracted From 30

Some Kind Of Love 32

Regarding Our Children 33

A Sweeping Kind Of Love 35

Cocoon Of Protection 37

Thoughts 40

Little Children 43

PREFACE

Blue Jungle is composed of satires, poems, and thoughts that comes from a quiet place, a still small voice place.

I hope these words on paper will affect you as I have been propelled to write them from my heart and transfer them into this exquisite book of words.
These words are from cumulative years at different times and in sundry places.
A cumulative explosion, some of wisdom, some of wishful thinking, and some of the exactness.

Thank you so very much for allowing me into your hearts and may the grace of God always, always, and forever be in your favor.

"Today if you would hear his voice"

HEBREWS 3:7

Sincerely

Nadolyn H. Robinson

TRANSLUCENT

Walked upon a clear, shining vein of the sun,
beaming its magnificent strength upon my face
as my eyes searched for its existence and beyond.

Each vein standing against itself
and on its own,
projecting its own strength
without permission.

I stand wistfully
experiencing this wisdom,
exhaling pure life,
realizing
I must first inhale!

Am I translucent?
Am I so visible?
Does each vein represent a road I must take?
or a road to be taken
to connect to the mainstream of the stem?
The root?
Can I travel that far?
go the distance?

I see straight into the sun.
I see straight into me.
I see straight into transparency

It pulls me like gravity, like sand, a million pieces of me,
an individual core of something
unexplainable but desirable.
I need no one's permission to be myself,
or to be me.
I am as translucent as the sun and it's power upholds me
I live through the veins of the sun
because of this power
I am
Translucent!

Is the air I breathe important to me?
Can I transport myself into the vein of the sun
as oxygen to a leaf?
Can I sit under the veins of this sun
and absorb its power of composure?
Is this a portal of survival to a sea of wisdom?

Or a sea of transport,
Or a sea of transparency,
Or a sea of transfiguration?
Of this that I see?

Have I been blinded by things, sight and sound?
Am I saved by grace or mercy?
Or wisdom and innocence?

What propels me
to a deep conversation and expectations?
What propels me
to fish for answers?
What propels me
to know when to seek and when to be still?

There is a quiet peace within
which prevents one from speaking
or even a hope
that a resolved answer awaits,
and can break into something
that we can touch, feel and taste!

I take a deep breath,
a deep, deep breath,
exhale power and sustenance sublime.

The veins of my innocence
is wrapped around the veins of that sun
which has carried me into an abyss of glory,
contentment and containment.

I eagerly await to see how my beginning catches up with my end
as I turn my face to see those veins in the sun
that helped me and prepared me on this road
that I traveled and arrived
under those many, many miles
I so wistfully endured
Nevertheless
I am
Translucence!

THE COLOR OF LOVE

Hebrews 11th Chapter of the Bible states,
now Faith is being sure of what we hope for
and certain of what we do not see,

The beginning of faith, and by faith,
we understand that the Universe was formed at God's command
so that what is seen was not made out of what was visible

> love is a common denominator
> for the settling of things
> for denoting things
> for denouncing hate
> and the first product of the beginning of time as we know it

Abraham,
when called to go to a place
where he would receive his inheritance,
obeyed and went,
even though he did not know where he was going.

> love is a common denominator
> for the settling of things,
> for denoting things,
> for denouncing hate
> and the first product of the beginning of time as we know it

Enoch,
was taken from this life
he did not experience death,
he could not be found

and without faith
it is impossible to please God,
because anyone who comes to him must believe that he exists
and that he rewards those who earnestly seek him by faith.

    love is a common denominator
    for the settling of things,
    for denoting things,
    for denouncing hate
    and the first product of the beginning of time as we know it

Faith is invisible and born out of love
Faith is invincible
Faith is love.

Love is invisible
Love is invincible
Love is colorless

the deduction that

God is invisible
God is invincible
God is colorless
he has no color agenda
he just is
love has no color agenda

it's just is

so the color of love
is the color of faith
is the color of God.
GOD IS COLORLESS
because he is faith and love,

all invisible, all invincible

ALL IN ONE!

And what more needs to be said!

HE JUST IS!!

THE LAZARUS EFFECT

Mary and Martha loved Jesus
Lazarus laid in the grave for 4 days
Sickness was not unto death but to glorify the son of God
whatsoever we will ask of God, he will give it.
Jesus wept.

Take ye away the stone.

Raising our minds and our hearts to take a stand for injustice,
The right to bear arms is in the Constitution and so many people
like to quote this constitutional right, but what about the right
to fight for injustice, the right to be free, the right to bear arms
for equality with the right to love one another.
There's a lot of power in the freedom of speech to bear arms
but also to bear love.
It should be our constitutional right to love and to be loved
but yet we rather stay buried with hatred and dishonor
and call it our constitutional right to bear anything
but the actual truth.
There is forgiveness which results from Love,
There is honor which results from Love,
There is hope which also results from Love,
but we as a people, a human race continue to be selfish
and want to hurt one another and call it constitutional.
Where is the Lazarus effect, why can't we arise out of the depths
of our own hatred and arise with the hope of some, even a sliver
of hope to try and love and show kindness and think of others first.

Why is the freedom that we have been given to live in a country
that projects and produces so much hate that it's unbearable!
There is an old saying "why can't we just all get along?"
It sounds corny, but a very true statement.

Why can't we try?
Why can't we hope for the best for ourselves and for others?
Why?

Like a Shepherd he will lead us.

We are not ourselves, we have been bought with a price,
and one day we will see either the harm we have caused
to one another or the Lazarus effect of not unto death
but to glorify the son of God!

Take ye away the stone!

We are imprisoned in our minds
take ye away the stone.

We are lost and not found
take ye away the stone

We are hampered without defeat
take ye away the stone

We are unpolished and imprisoned
take ye away the stone

We are ridiculed
take ye away the stone.

We have been hidden behind a stone, a wall of injustice
a wall of persecution, constantly
belittling ourselves, limiting ourselves, hurting ourselves because of
selfishness and circumstances that do not define

who we are and who we are meant to be!

We must rise against all hate!
and act with love in our hearts and with common sense.
This is that Lazarus effect for the people,
be who you are created to be, all people, all mankind!

Enter into his gates!

PLEASE TAKE AWAY THE STONE!

LEADER BANDIT

Place your shoes under the bed
Wrap your soul from end to end
With wisdom of a different color.

HEAVEN IS REAL

I know heaven is real
When moments of life gets tough

I Pray

Any situations become
Any situations
Are all situations,

Become easier somehow
I can't see first the smoothing out of
But when it happens,
It happens!

I know Heaven is real because

I Pray

When moments bring pain of hurt and despair

I pray

When time erases the fear
Of the unknown
It's because

I pray

Not of my own hand or volitions of sight unseen
Not because of what someone else said so,
Or the fear of what someone said
It's because

I pray

Prayer changes things
This I know because the bible said so
Because I have witnessed the change
Because I heard about faith

I tested faith
I enveloped faith
I swallowed faith
I engulped faith
I preserved faith
I stood on faith
I was promised faith
I tackled faith
The Holy Bible cannot lie
It stands on it's own word
It is revelation to the ears of peace and the beginning of justice.
Promises upon promises
The power of The Holy Spirit makes it so
Of this that I see
And of this that I know
Prayer changes things

Heaven is Real!

PERIOD!

BLUE JUNGLE

Blue Jungle is a statement,
a feeling,
an attitude.
It can be about love, hurt, pain,
tenderness, excitement, hope, color, beauty,
struggle, determination, wisdom and

poverty of spirit.....

Blue Jungle is love,
love for someone who doesn't always love back,
But has the capacity to love
without knowing it.
Love without borders,
without expectations,
but open- ended.

Blue Jungle is not fancy and
doesn't require fancy things to be a part of its core,
It's fluid
both in and out.

Blue Jungle is an entity that flows,
captures what needs to be captured,
put a stamp on it!
It moves forward,
always forward,
never ever backwards!

Blue Jungle is Maudie Lewis the painter,
(He was looking for a woman to clean his house and found the capacity to love and even love himself.)

Blue Jungle is Misty Copeland The Principal Ballerina
(finding her destiny without a crutch)

BRAVO!!

Blue Jungle is conflict versus resolution!

Finding your destiny without a crutch!

DULCE

Dulce - to make sweet; soothe
Dulia - the reverence according to saints and angels

As I opened the door to this sunny cafe named Dulce which is French for sweets as I understand it, I was immediately drawn to its ambiance and simplicity.
As I enter this cafe I immediately notice to my left, a large sweet looking dessert sitting on a plate being encased by the sun casting a shadow over it's owner, a gentleman of unique appearance.

This man's appearance was evidence of a rugged and hard life, starting with his many layered time-worn clothes, tangled hair and beard, with skin darkened by so many days in the sun that it's hard to tell what his natural color is.
His features are not Anglo Saxon, but I can see beauty underneath the grim, and it was flowing from within.
I tried to continue watching him without staring while standing in line waiting for my opportunity to order a coffee and dessert but it was a challenge. I was drawn to this gentle man for reasons unknown to me.

The cafe is filled with people enjoying their morning coffee, dessert, etc. Although I see them, I am captivated by this gentleman.
I take a seat not far away from him and notice how the sun is casting it's shine through the very large picture window where he is seated.
I sugar my latte and began to eat my croissant while pulling out a book to read as I'm continually drawn to this man.
I periodically look up at him in the time-worn many layered clothes, tangled beard, deep in thought and I wonder what his thoughts are.

*My thoughts are on nothing specific, but this gentleman didn't move or make a sound, he just looked straight ahead through the
sunlit window. I didn't want to continue staring, so I decided to attempt to read my book but I am unable to concentrate fully.*

I saw him as he stood to leave and I quietly wished he wasn't leaving but he left anyway.
This was such a strange encounter because as soon as he left I missed his presence.

Nadolyn H. Robinson

JUDGEMENT

Grate, grate, grate
Fireplace this to injustice
Reputed demonstration of freedom
Wet down like dogs in the street
Unwelcome and adorn
Annie, get your gun. Get your gun, get your gun,
Keep them on the run, on the run, on the run
Make them cry out and escape to the sun
Bottoms up wayward

Standing like Hacksaw Ridge,
standing by the good and righteous principles
Of God we love
Where are those men and women of God anymore?
There are a few but this demonstration of courage and peace should be greater, even larger
than life, but they are very far and very, very behind the lines
They are definitely few and far, so far between!
Knowing you are called and here on this earth for a reason and purpose but yet you bow down
to cowardness, criticism and just plain wrong and full of injustice!
You have no backbone; it appears that you have no backbone.
You definitely do not act like you have faith in GOD for which you stated and stand in the pulpit on a regular basis declaring that God is your God and that he is a God of love
but yet
You do not act, or your actions are not actions of love and this seems to be okay with you?

What kind of rationalization do you convince yourself when you lay your head down to sleep with?

There is a scripture in the bible regarding judgment that states you cry ABBA father, but your
heart is far away from me!
Extreme to extremist
Lions to lambs
Trading for the lesser of the two evils
Lean not to the right or the left.
0.06 degrees of separation
Things of thought
Things of promise
Things of direction
Matthew 7: 21,22, and 23

Read it!

WHO'S FOOL/ YOU'RE FOOL/ NO FOOL YOU'RE GAME/ NO NAME /PERIOD

Judge me not as a fool
For you might fall
In love with me,
And as
The truth surface, you'll find me
Not a fool.
The essence of my existence is far superior
To your game,
Therefore your thinking is like a man
With no name.
God didn't make no fools
Period.

IT IS TRUE

It is true,

There is a time and a place for everything under the sun,

a time for you

and

a time for me.

We are a splendor in the grass

a raisin in the sun

a glory in the flower

and

miles to go before we sleep,

and

miles to go before we sleep.

Wait for your time

It will surely come.

FORTITUDE

Find the road that you must travel on
Find the road that you must live out
Contribute to peace and healing.
Allowing the possibility of the transformation of the soul.

Choose to use priceless childlike faith
Simplicity of truth
Be a rock of revelation and support.
Extinguish untruths.

Modify, modify, modify

Employ relentless the integrity of life
Allow the possibility of the transformation of the soul!
Reaching the pinnacles porches of
Rhythm, rhyme, and reason.

SOMEDAY

Someday you will have to look beyond the crowded room

Someday you will have to look beyond the crowded room

Someday you will have to hear within the crowded room

Someday you will have to hear within the crowded room

Someday you will have to walk into the crowded room

and listen, look, and believe that you are
unique,
gifted
and loved!

Can you hear my voice?
Can you feel my heart?

CAN YOU?

WAITING FOR THE SEASON YET TO COME

Waiting for the season yet to come
Delivered by the hand of Grace
Unwelcomed and adorned.

Pulsating strong with spiritual ease
Given this race only to please.

Who knocks at the door of their inner tuition?
No one we know, but we're willing to listen.

Can I come?
Can I come in?
Are you there?
Will you let me in?

Are you ready?
Are you sure?
Can you hear me?
Is there one?

What keeps you from searching?
Are you afraid?
Are you lonely?
Do you need another day?

Can I help you?
Can I come?
Tell me, are you ready?
Is there one?

One among you so great and full of life?

Can you measure?
Can you count?
What have we here?
Time is running out!

Am I here?
Am I here to stay?

Yes I am!
Can I come?
Can I come today?

Waiting for the season
Yet to come
Delivered by the hand of Grace
Unwelcome and adorned!

SILENCE

Silence

Each tear I cry reminds me of why it's so quiet
What becomes of a broken heart?

Hurt brings joy, smiles bring tears
Refuge breeds freedom.

Silence

Silence captures love
What evidence pools around the imagination
To conquer the evidence of an infatuation?

Silence

In syncopated time
Beginnings and endings
Endings and beginnings

And hearts once empty
Fill with four letters words
Hope
Love
Life

Silence

Reborn-Rebirth-Rejuvenated
From the depth of silence
And unformed words
Sing a brilliant truth
Recognizable to sages and lost souls

Silence embraces me
It tortures me!
It envelops me!

Undeniable love
Drips from forehead to breast
Drenched in the meadow of truth

Fear cast out like exposed thieves
And the deafening wail of silence
Hums the song of joy
The song of life
The song of love

Witnesses allowed to ponder
The powerful footprints that are left upon the earth.
Silence captures love
    because
Death has no sting!

Silence

A well beloved person knows
In each moment of embrace
We rise to the occasion of true love

    because
Perfect love cast out all fear
Promises upon promises
Kept and unkept

Traveled away, far away
Until my true love returns to me
And blow me away!

Silence

Each tear I cry reminds me of why it's so quiet

So why don't you stay until
It's time for you to go
don't cry for me!
don't cry for me!
Rejoice with me!

        because

My true love has come for me

Silently

CRUCIFIED

        CRUCIFIED

HUNG ON THE CROSS

                CHRISTMAS LIGHTS
                PEACE
                TRANSGRESSIONS
                HOPE
                LOVE
                DO NOT WEEP FOR ME

FORGIVENESS OF SINS

                BARING ARMS
                FAITH

SPACE

S- space, space, space
   broken up, humanized, prepared and reported
P- place for space to cooperate with
A- after the fact, after the
C- call, after the consciousness of
E- everyone and everything and all.

GIVE
ME
SPACE
SO
I
MAY HAVE PEACE!

WORDS OF WISDOM EXTRACTED FROM
(A PATRIOT'S HANDBOOK INTRODUCED
BY CAROLINE KENNEDY)

You need all kinds of intellect to
Interlink the wisdom that's needed
To reach those who are calling out for help
Or an answer to something.

To get freedom you have to give freedom
Great responsibility and great accountability
Happiness of future generations

And…

A free nation has the right to expect
To look into the leaders
To take the lead of a stimulating effort

In that…

Men do not live by bread alone, but by
Wisdom and every word proceeded
Out by the mouth of God

New order of things…

Our strength is our unity of purpose
There can be no end except victory
Faith in freedom under the guidance of God.

Such as…

DR. King's I Have a Dream Speech,
John F. Kennedy's Inaugural Speech of 1961
George Washington Carver's many contributions

And…

From the effective lines of the
Declaration of Independence
We hold this truth to be self-evident
that all men, all men, all men,
Are created equal
It is never too late to give up our prejudices
Today, an inquisitor
Faith in the ultimate justice of things.

SOME KIND OF LOVE

Some kind of love when we allow each other to fall into a pit of
PERDITION__ KNOWINGLY

Some kind of love when we allow each other to be taken
ADVANTAGE OF__ KNOWINGLY

Some kind of love when we allow each other to hate one and
another and NOT CORRECT THEM__KNOWINGLY

Some kind of love when we allow each other to cheat, to destroy,
TO LIE__KNOWINGLY

AND SOME KIND OF LOVE WHEN WE TAKE ADVANTAGE OF EACH OTHER'S WEAKNESS'S KNOWINGLY AND NOT DETER THEM TO WHAT IS RIGHT.

SHAME ON US ___KNOWINGLY

REGARDING OUR CHILDREN

What is a mother to do?
What is a father to do?

Regarding bullying....

Regarding our children returning home to
us safe and in a sound mind...

When the child doesn't come home from school..

That we must find a way to return our children
home and assure ourselves that once we send
our children out to school or social events
that they will return to us whole...

Guns versus children.... Are guns more important than children?..
I would imagine even people with guns want
their children to return home safely.

Children going out...

to school having to confront bullying …
or
mental illness or stress related incidents..

not returning home....

Children going out...
to school ....
become injured or illness at school...

Not returning home....

Children going out in cars....

because of accidents prompted by many reasons and non-awareness...

not returning home...

Children going out..

NOT RETURNING HOME...

A SWEEPING KIND OF LOVE

I met a man named Jimbo
His hair was white as snow
And everywhere his wallet went
I was sure to go!

He took me to the store one day and
Bought me rings and things,
And asked me if I would marry him,
But there was just one thing.

I said what's that Jimbo?
What do you have to say?

He said marry me tomorrow
And forgive me for today.

Forgive you for today I say?
Yes forgive me for today,
Because today I must find a bride,
Before to death, I lay.
Before to death you lay?
What kind of talk is this I say?

Jimbo bowed his head and asked
If he could have a kiss before he went away.
Of course I said to Jimbo,
Yes you may have a kiss
Before your death bed you lay.
But what am I to do on each passing day?
My fair lady he said

You must fight the fight of injustice
For all mankind everywhere and
Give them wise advice to prepare.
To prepare I say? Prepare for what?

Jimbo raised his head, and with
Piercing eyes said,
There is a sweeping kind of love on it's way
A sweeping kind of love!!!

COCOON OF PROTECTION

On an unbeaten path to nowhere we find ourselves caught up in the rapture of delight placed in a cocoon of protection with significant love for one another brought on by unselfishness.

Like the oval nut falling from the oak tree endowed with various shapes, uneaten and sprinkled with mayhem given languishly to the possums of beach and baths. We witness the reality of cares as being open ended, but the gist of reality is closed(the essential points at least) the understanding of what's real is closed like the rat-a –tat-tat of the guns of Navarone, the blissful mist absorbs all of its contents and elements of this that I see. Redundancy of nerves like gas vapors edging its way into the scene of an ever evolving tree-like substance, like honey.

Where is the misfortune of understanding of solitude brought on by a magnificent power and the liability to believe in the power of oneself, ourselves. This remarkable entity of real power within itself is not one to overcome, but one to endure. Given the remarkable attitude of such a vice, we are impeccably sure of ourselves. A cocoon of protection hardened by our ability to please others head on and without platitude can/should show off our talents without retribution. How can this be a popular stance in this repertoire of solitude given for comparison to upchuck and beatdown tree upon root, root upon part, subservience to an entity of an open awareness to the credit of any and all things. Production of greatness with clarity, magnificent power, retribution, and purposes of such promiscuity of power is essential for awareness.

The acorn that sits in the tree is unwavering or unaware of its solitude, it just exists and the universe around it gives it its place, its growth is from a seedling and the sun, and water has given its shape and existence.

The heart and its heartbeat are one, we and the creator are one, somehow we have missed that concept and forgotten that we were created by something greater than ourselves. The acorn is part of that greatness. Its evolution revolutionizes the simplest part of a seedling to a tree.

What derivative surmounts the power of oneself, to look, inspect, retrieve, act and become subservient.

Come on, what are you thinking? Can this be what it's all about? Such enviousness, jealousy, powerlessness, can I not submit to these entities? What's required to make a change?

We are required to make a change.

THE INTERPRETATION

I sat in a seat on a bus today, it was the first single seat behind the bus driver and I noticed a small plaque that read "this seat is dedicated to the memory of Rosa Parks, who took a seat on a bus in Montgomery, Alabama and changed the course of American History."

To change the course of American History without prejudice, but born to a world that denied her, her inalienable rights, but yet was created like you and me to that particular entity and responsibility without knowing the course that lies ahead, but being true to herself without fear, and with a conscience of divine ordination, protected as the acorn, hard shell and steady, sitting alone, unnoticed until the right time.

It is true, there is a time and place for everything under the sun, a time for you and a time for me. Wait for your time, it will surely come. We are a splendor in the grass, a raisin in the sun, a glory in the flower, and miles to go before we sleep, and miles to go before we sleep.

THOUGHTS

An idea or opinion produced by thinking...Or occurring suddenly in the mind.

Have you ever thought about what you are thinking about at any given time? Or have you just stopped and listened to your thoughts?

I have often wondered if this process happened to many people. Sometimes I try to focus on exactly what I am thinking, and my mind will wander to thoughts of what to do on vacation, or what to wear, or how much money this or that will cost. Although this sounds like good thought provoking ideas, the question still eluded me as to why am I thinking these thoughts at this particular time? I'm not necessarily in a relaxed, easy chair environment.

I'm at work where my thoughts should be directed on work issues.

I'm the type of person who likes a challenge, so one day I decided to try and evaluate what I was thinking about at this particular time! So I sat down and wrote down what my thoughts were. Mind you, I don't have a degree in Philosophy, but I pay attention as to what is in my head and as to why things happen as they do. Some of this is curiosity and some of it is related to a natural scientific mind.

I was in the library the other day, walking down each aisle, not really knowing what I wanted to read. I looked at the title of some books and shrugged my shoulders and kept walking. I suddenly stopped and picked out a book by Maya Angelou, A Song Flung Up To Heaven. I came home, entered the living room, turned on the television and I heard Oprah introducing Maya Angelou with a birthday celebration and there she was with her new book, the same one I had just picked out at the library! What a coincidence I thought? The timing was perfect and I enjoyed the book even more, because I believed there was a connection.

Have you ever gone to the movies and watched it for its content instead of its entertainment value? I have always wondered how writers choose their subject matter and topic. The movie The Matrix is a perfect example! There are so many elements to that movie that's unbelievable! That is definitely a movie out of the box, and out of the norm. I enjoyed it tremendously! This movie really made me think about a lot of possibilities! What if that type of experience is possible, even in the slightest or remote of an idea. What kind of powerful thinking that will produce! To believe in yourself and your accomplishments to the extent that you can't be stopped stopped or touched?

In the role of Lawrence Fishburne as Orpheus and Keanu Reeves as the chosen one, who was given a choice to choose between the blue pill or the red pill, which would show him a difference and a challenge from the life he was already living, a life of mundane repetition ...Of course he chose the pill that would turn his life upside down, and after that things took off in a whirlwind! Well I was blown away by that movie. One particular part that caught my attention was when Orpheus told him that he would be able to stop bullets and that he couldn't be killed, so what's to fear? Well I thought that meant he would stop the bullets like in the comic book of Superman, where the bullets just bounce off of his chest. I thought that was powerful enough in an imaginary world, but the time came for the chosen one to see the power he had over the evil guy. Well the gun was aimed at him and the bullets left the gun and STOPPED!!! While he stood there and appeared fearless, the bullets just dropped to the floor! That just blew me away!!!

I immediately began to think where such thoughts and ideas to write such things come from? All I am trying to say is that the ideas that writers and producers have must originate for a reason, and that something is to give us insight to stretch our imagination and give ourselves a chance to explore possibilities that can make a difference. Just the thought of something greater than ourselves can initiate such a powerful motivation of unlimited consequences. I know it's fiction but any idea that can give away to something positive and concrete can't be all bad! You think?

Sidney Poiter gave a statement in an article regarding his career and stated "I launched a journey more incredible than I could have imagined, to a destiny written in a time before I came, by hands other than my own".

LITTLE CHILDREN

Ease up little children

Let's pray

What's on your mind?

Ease up little children

Time is on your side

Ease up little children

Pray what's on your mind

Ease up little children

Jesus is coming back!

Rise up little children

God is on your side

Rise up little children

It's time

It's your time

to bring

Christ back

In your time!